HISTORY OF SWEDEN

A BRIEF OVERVIEW FROM BEGINNING TO END

HISTORY ENCOUNTERS

Bonus Downloads

*Get Free Books with **<u>Any Purchase</u>** History Shorts*

Every purchase comes with a FREE download!

History of Sweden

A Brief History from Beginning to the End

History Shorts

CONTENTS

Chapter One

Introduction

Sweden's history is an interesting one. Their ties with Denmark and Norway go back to the early times of Scandinavia,a group of countries in Northern Europe. Because of their geographical relations, their histories are intricately intertwined. You can't discuss one without the other. So, you will first learn about the prehistoric history of Scandinavia and how they used to live, particularly in the Stone and Bronze Ages.

Of course, what is Sweden's history without the topic of the Vikings and Christianity? The Vikings, one of the last violent pagan groups, were seafaring men who terrorized different settlements in the name of their gods. However, when Christianity first came to Sweden, they were surprisingly very accepting and even allowed St. Ansgar, the archbishop who first introduced Christianity to the Swedes, to preach among them. However, they soon became wary, and some had renounced Christianity. Soon enough, the Crusades started, and through the military expeditions supported by the Latin Church, Sweden did convert, albeit against its will.

But the Crusades weren't their only battle. The enemies lurked closer in the form of the Kalmar Union between Norway, Denmark, and Sweden. The alliance unified the three countries under a single governing monarch that kept peace for some years. However, like all alliances, there were inequalities that shook its foundations. Denmark's superiority, even though it was Sweden that initiated the whole Union, put Norway down the hierarchy. The in-fighting sparked when the Union decided on the fate of Norway. With the country struggling, either Sweden or Denmark wanted it. Then the king of Denmark, Christian II, also wished to take Sweden for himself, invading it twice during his reign. The first was a failure, but the second one established the Dane stronghold in Swedish territory. He also was the instigator behind the Massacre in Stockholm. In the end, however, the Swedish people were able to take back their kingdom. These conflicts ultimately dissolved the Union.

Have you ever wondered what Sweden's role in the World Wars was? They tried their best to stay out of it and be neutral. However, as you know, wars are not that simple. Publicly, they are neutral. Internally, however, some of them sided with Germany in both wars because of their sympathetic ties with the country. But things turned around during World

War II when they found out about Germany's plans to invade them, and so the Swedes deceived the Germans and broke their agreement. In the end, Sweden became stronger after the wars.

If you look at Sweden's history, they made so much progress in terms of agriculture, politics, and societal ways. From simple fishing and hunting, they started animal breeding and production in agriculture and began processing animal by-products, such as milk to make dairy products. They also started taking care of their forests and using their mines. The most significant thing about their agriculture is their water system that allowed them to successfully harness hydroelectric power.

Meanwhile, the Swedish parliament used to be helmed by the Riksdag. Louis De Geer later reformed its four estates into two chambers. Of course, there were some who opposed this, but in the end, it was passed. Also, as usual, men were the predominant gender in all things political. So women fought for their rights and were eventually permitted to have a say in Sweden's political landscape.

Swedish social progress didn't always lead a straight road. The first item on its list of issues was women's rights and what is owed to them. Then there is the Temperance Movement that dealt with the rampant alcoholism in the country. The last is about the question of labor. Sweden, like most countries, has exploited its workers, inciting countrywide strikes. The economic disruptions eventually led the government to concede to their demands.

Now, what's history without art and discoveries? Swedish people have cultivated a rich literary and art scene. There are several writers who make hymns, not just poetry, and countless more painters who used nature as their muse. And let's not forget the inventions some of the most brilliant Swedish people made that revolutionized transportation today.

Chapter Two
Scandinavia

We are supposed to talk about Sweden; however, Scandinavia's history is Sweden's as well. So, it is best to start on the history of Scandinavia as a whole to better understand the events that unfolded in Sweden and those of its neighboring countries that undoubtedly affected Sweden.

Scandinavia is a territory comprising three countries in northern Europe: Sweden, Denmark, and Norway. This is to be differentiated with the Nordic countries that include Finland, Greenland, and Iceland as well. Due to their geological position, they share many things in their culture, and their history is intertwined with one another. This set of countries have a rich history together.

Most developments, such as the arrival of the first settlers and the introduction of cultures, started in Denmark, then it slowly spread to Sweden and Norway. At the start of the Preboreal Period, the human population grew, and since people settled near bodies of water, most of them engaged in fishing and hunting. The Neolithic Age, also known as the New Stone Age, in Scandinavia started in this period, and animal husbandry (animal breeding) and cultivation were developed with the advent of stone tools.

The early settlers in Scandinavia were hunters who mainly hunted for reindeer meat. Hunters used the landscape to their advantage. The land was where they found their main source of food and materials for their housing. As they stayed longer, they became hunters of the seas, and found more ways to adapt. As they traveled further up north, they left a trail for the present-day archeologists to trace and study. Because of this, they discovered the Hensbacka culture of western Sweden, the Fosna of the Western and Southern Norwegian coast, and the Kosma culture of Finnmark (Norway).

Animal breeding, however helpful, wasn't the main livelihood of the early settlers, although it may have become increasingly important due to the fast changes in climate. They went to some lengths to do this. In fact, they would cause forest fires to clear the way for the breeding land. Because of cultivation and pastoralism, the people formed some social order as a way to divide the labor. There would be people in storage, the farmers, and of course, the people involved in the production (from the farm to the warehouse). Each village's size grew, resulting in the elevated importance of animal husbandry and cultivation in southern Scandinavia. The Bronze Age started around 1800 BC. While there wasn't much difference from the Stone Age in terms of culture, society, economy, and demographics, there were still some fundamental advances during the Bronze Age. Archeologists found that the industrial aspect of Scandinavia has changed. There was also a good shift in the exchange markets. While animal cultivation and agriculture were at the forefront of Scandinavian commerce in this age, there were now metal artifacts and gold. Accessories such as rings, bracelets, and necklaces were made, so were weapons and defense armor. During this time, geographical lines were more tangible, but there was no competition over resources, land, and chiefdom or leadership.

In southern Scandinavia, Sweden's Bronze Age culture was preserved through rock carvings. They contain the records of human civilization and seafaring rituals that they used to perform. There would also be representations of human body parts and nature itself. These archeological artifacts gave archeologists a glimpse of the agricultural lives of Scandinavian people.

Later on, a change in the economy of Scandinavia had its early settlers expand their territories even further to keep up. They established themselves on the Finnish coastline of Kiukainen. This made them quasi-colonizers, albeit, not on a big scale compared to other aggressive colonizers in the world at that time.

In the Iron Age, Scandinavia grew separate from Europe, creating a border. This age introduced new political, economic, and cultural orders. Evidence of the start of the Metal Age was first found in Finnmark. Populations all started out small and then spread to the Swedish Norrland, where they established more permanent housing and returned to hunting for sustenance. This is how they paid for dowries and other necessities and luxuries.

However, since Scandinavia was divided, there were different takes on how the pre-Roman Iron Age actually played out. The Southern part of Scandinavia, which encompassed Denmark, Sweden, and Norway, had other agricultural effects. The three lands shared more similarities compared to the Nordic countries. For example, their stable settlement pattern around farmlands and their culture are identical with one another.

As the difference became more stark, the Three Northern Kingdoms rose:

Denmark, Norway, and Sweden.

Chapter Three
The Vikings and The Introduction of
Christianity

The Vikings, referred to as "noble savages," where the last great pagan soldiers before Christianity came into play. There are several theories as to why the Vikings came to be. Some books say that these people did not want to follow their chiefs, so they took to the seas and became sea-kings. Other texts say this is their method of conquering other lands. In summary, however, the Vikings are tyrants, no matter which origin story is the truest. The Swedish Viking Expeditions, called "Eastway," mostly focused on the southern and eastern shores of the Baltic Sea. The usual route was the Gulf of Finland, up the River Neva, and across Lake Ladoga, then by another river course south to Lake Ilmen. The Black Sea was where a lot of the Viking ships sailed toward. The goal was to get to Constantinople for the treasures they believed were there. The Vikings also dabbled in trading goods, mostly furs.

There were many stories about the Vikings who had gone Eastway. Their travels were written down in runic inscriptions. However, most stories were written past the Viking Age, so there is a question of reliability.

The religion of the Viking Age was paganism or polytheism. They worshipped multiple higher beings that controlled different aspects of life and nature. This religion was closely intertwined with their culture, unlike Christianity. The gods they worshipped came from Norse Mythology, including Thor, Odin, Heimdall, and so on.

The first person to introduce Christianity to Sweden was St. Ansgar who was born in Northern France as an orphan. At first, he was far from a saint until he had a dream, a vision of the Virgin Mary that made him change his ways. St. Ansgar went to Sweden around the year 830AD. But as he approached the coast, he was attacked by the Vikings. By some chance, he survived, and when he arrived at Sweden's chief city, he received a friendly welcome from King Björn. St. Ansgar was appointed the archbishop for the three Scandinavian lands.

When everyone assembled, there was a lot of talk against Christianity. That was until one old man got up and said, "Hear me, king and people, many of us know that the Christian's God can give great help to those who put their trust in him, for this has often been witnessed in perils at sea and other dangers. Why, then, should we reject what we know to be useful? When our gods are unfavorable, it is well to have the favor of this God, who is ever ready to help those who call upon him." These words persuaded the people to let St. Ansgar preach Christianity in their land. The king gave land for the construction of his church and appointed St. Ansgar as the priest.

When St. Ansgar died, it took years for the preachers of Christianity to come back to Sweden. While the first Christian king was Olof Skötkonung, his people were still largely pagans. Sweden's conversion to Christianity was a slow process, as it took much work to convince the Vikings. The missionaries got creative, and they incorporated some of their pagan teachings into their teachings, claiming that Jesus Christ might be a different version of their god, Baldur.

In 1070, the Christian monk Adam of Bremen arrived in Sweden, and because of him, the nobles were converted, along with a large population of the country. Soon enough, people who didn't convert to Christianity were forced to due to a law that rendered paganism illegal.

Towards the end of the eleventh century, people in Europe started becoming aggressive in spreading their religion. A lot of Christian warriors invaded pagan territories in the name of Christianity, destroying multiple cities in the process.

The Swedish Crusades turned against the pagans of Finland. The king then, King Eric, led a crusade against the Finns and demanded they accept holy baptism. When they refused, the Swedish army attacked and forced the survivors to be baptized. In a way, the Crusaders have become the new Vikings.

King Eric was killed and was deemed a martyr to the cause. Other Finnish tribes continued to defy the Crusades. They had to "lock up the Lake Mälar," meaning they had to build a fortress around Stockholm. The Swedish Crusades weren't satisfied with just mere defense, so they continued their attacks on the Finns.

The Swedish Crusades continued from the reign of Eric the Lisp and the Lame, assisted by Birger Jarl (Earl Birger). The whole crusade went on to the Tavastians in central Finland. Everyone had to accept baptism, or else they were killed.

Chapter Four
The Period of the Union

The Kalmar Union, established by Queen Margaret, was an attempt to unify the three kingdoms (Norway, Denmark, and Sweden) to become one Scandinavian kingdom. Individually, the kingdoms were weak. But together, they would accumulate enough power to fend off threatening rivals.

However, Queen Margaret was aware that Denmark seemed to be at the forefront of this Union, which is expected since Denmark was the wealthiest and most populated of the three. She decided to appoint Danish nobles as the bailiffs of the Swedish nobles. Because of Denmark's supremacy, the Union was hardly noticeable. But Queen Margaret somehow made it work, as she had the respect of everyone. However, when she died, things changed.

Eric of Pomerania, the nephew of Queen Margaret, was a German, and this caused some unsettling feelings. There were a lot of Germans in Sweden who became the king's bailiffs to rule the Swedish people. Finally, the Danes (people of Denmark) and Germans rose to power and started to rule over powerful parts of the kingdom.

Engelbert Engelbertsson was a Swedish mine owner who took action against this tyranny. When King Eric refused to hear him out, the miners and peasants of Dalecarlia and Westmanland rose and forced the enemies out of their castles. This caused a ripple effect as other peasants in the country also started uprisings. The uprisings came to the point where Engelbertsson persuaded the king's council (a group of nobility) to renounce their loyalty to King Eric. This gave birth to the first Swedish Riksdag, or Parliament. In this meeting, the peasants urged Engelbertsson to be the regent of Sweden, and it was sustained. This was the first time the peasants had a say in the politics of their land. Before Engelbertsson died, he was able to unite all classes and provinces in the name of the fatherland.

The peasants were left without a leader when Engelbertsson died. The Lords tried to take matters into their own hands, but they were now divided: the Swedish party that desired a native king versus the Union Party. The head of the Swedish party is a nobleman named Karl Knutsson

Bonde. He became the king of Sweden in the year 1448. However, during this time, the Danes have chosen a German as their king, Christian I.

Now that Sweden and Denmark crowned their new kings, where does Norway go? Due to long civil struggles, Norway became too weak to stand on its own. They did not have an Engelbertsson to help defend the peasants. The two kings wanted Norway. They agreed to a joint meeting of Swedish and Danish council members to decide and conclude that Christian I will have Norway.

However, while King Karl busied himself in Norway's affairs, an archbishop, Jöns Bengtsson Oxenstierna, was planning to grab the power from him. It came to the point where he stopped being an archbishop and planned a coup to overthrow King Karl. He succeeded in his plan, and King Karl fled as he was both betrayed and wounded.

Bengtsson extorted the people, and he kept asking for taxes so much so that he was nicknamed "bottomless-empty-purse" by the peasants. However, his reign didn't last long because the peasants drove him out. That's when King Karl was finally called back to the throne.

After King Karl came Sten Sture the Elder. At this time, Christian I was determined to grab the throne of Sweden for himself. He attempted an attack at Brunkeberg Ridge. He failed, but Christian I was far from giving up.

Christian II of Denmark was the grandson of Christian I, who had the same craving for the crown of Sweden. Sten Sture the Younger was the regent in Sweden at the same time Christian II was in power. Christian II's first attack on Sweden was in the summer of 1518. He came up to Stockholm with a large army. However, the peasant army defeated him, which was a quick win. They shifted gears and offered a peace negotiation with the Sten Sture the Younger. He, being innocent, of course, accepted. He was warned, though, and he took that into account. The deal was that Sten Sture the Younger would bring six Swedish nobles onto the ship of Christian II for safety. However, when the six nobles were sent to the Danish fleet, Christian II imprisoned them and returned to Denmark. For him, this was just the beginning.

Christian II made great preparations for his next attack on Sweden. When he returned with a huge army, the peasant warriors fought them as before. However, Sten Sture the Younger got injured at the start, leaving the military without a commander. So, Christian II's army prevailed, passcd Tiveden, and laid waste to Swealand. Despite Sten Sture the

Younger's injuries, he traveled to Stockholm, thinking that he must add defenses to the capital city. Sadly, he died on the trip back. His death sparked a fire inside the peasants, who fought back even harder. However, their attempts weren't enough.

Even though it seemed bleak, the people gathered around Christina Gyllenstierna, Sten Sture the Younger's wife. She assumed a position and fought back in the name of her husband. Because of her leadership, Christian II couldn't penetrate the capital. Though, he continued to fight. In the end, he promised to stop the war and still respect the law system if they surrendered. Finally, the capital was subdued, and Christian II was crowned the new Swedish King.

On the day of his coronation, Christian II made a devious plan with Gustav Trolle, an enemy of Sten Sture the Elder. Trolle was meant to demand Christian II's deposition, and all who agreed would be killed. The plan succeeded and the treasoners were killed in front of everyone at Stockholm's Great Square (also known as the Market). The widows of the men who were killed were imprisoned. This event was called the Massacre of Stockholm.

Meanwhile, a man has already made himself known as a knight against Christian II. A young leader for Swedish liberty was coming around. He is Gustavus Ericsson Vasa, one of the six nobles who were captured on Christian II's ship. After a year of imprisonment, he was able to escape and made his way back to Sweden in disguise. He met with his sister and her husband. They both went to Christian II's coronation despite Ericsson's warnings. And sadly, they died in the massacre. This lit a fire in Ericsson. He went back in disguise and made his way to Dalecarlia.

He went to Lake Siljan and persuaded the people of Dalecarlia to join him on his quest to overthrow Christian II. He used empathy to get other people to stand up, expressing his grief about the Stockholm Massacre, where he lost his sister. He reminded them of Engelbertsson and the Sture leaders. However, they did not join him, for they were tired of this constant war. Also, they were unaware of the bloodshed since it hadn't reached them. But then word did get to them, and they all rallied behind Ericsson, calling him the Commander of Dalecarlians.

After much training, Ericsson and his army made their way to Westmanland, and the Danes met them halfway for a battle in Vesterås. Ericsson won and continued on. However, they seemed to be losing during the battle at Stockholm. Thankfully, Christian II left because of another war with the Lübecks, leaving the capital city vulnerable.

The Riksdag in Strengnäs appointed Ericsson as King Gustavus I, and the victory was secured soon after that.

The abuse the Sweden people suffered from Eric of Pomerania, and Christian II can't be overlooked. So, after Gustavus I's battle, the Karmal Union was dissolved.

This is a picture of a Swedish Viking.

This is a picture of St. Ansgar.

Chapter Five
Natural Resources and Economy

We discussed that the people of Scandinavia did animal breeding, especially cattle breeding. It continued throughout the years and has reached a point of great prosperity. Science made sure of that. Breeding cattle was very adaptable to the ever-changing climate. At first, they had a gruesome method of starving the cattle during winter. This was how they would let the creatures die for meat. However, this practice was not only wrong but uneconomical, so they stopped.

Besides cattle breeding, the animals helped with the dairy industry of Sweden as well. Since the number of cows increased, so did the yield of milk. At first, Sweden couldn't produce enough butter for personal consumption. But now, the communities have established creameries across the country.

Forestry was another source of wealth for Sweden because of the good quality of its timber and other forest products. However, it wasn't always like that. Before, they would barely protect the forests, even creating forest fires to gain more agricultural or pastoral land. They used to cut down mature trees and saplings without thinking of planting new ones in their place. But they turned around, creating laws to protect the forests of Sweden. Cutting down trees was now illegal. If you were to cut one down, you would be required to plant another tree in its place.

The Falun Copper Mine was called "Sweden's treasury." Around the sixteenth to the seventeenth century, it was the richest copper mine in all of Europe. However, today it is almost exhausted of its treasure. Still, though, Sweden has an abundant supply of the best quality iron ore internationally.

We move into the Machine Age ushered in by James Watt in 1769 when machines began to revolutionize the industrial system of the world. However, the Machine Age reached Sweden at the beginning of the nineteenth century. An English mechanic, Samuel Owen, established himself in Stockholm. He created the first Swedish factory using steam power. After that, the domino effect began. The gathering and production of the natural resources were now powered by steam. Sweden has finally gotten over its handicap of having a lack of coal, since it now used hydropower to run its factories' production lines.

Trade has always been a part of Sweden's history. They have good trade relations with Germany and Poland because of their direct connection to Prussia's railroad system. Besides inland trading, the Swedish constructed the Göta Canal for their overseas trades. Furthermore, one of the most notable canals made was the Trollhätte Canal. On the Riksdag of 1809, it was decided that the work of connecting the Baltic Sea with the western side of the country should be continued. However, the costs of doing this were far greater than the first budget. So, they made adjustments for the construction of the Trollhätte Canal.

The person who brought in the railroad system to Sweden was Adolf von Rosen. Having studied the railroad problems of England, it was his ambition to put Sweden at the forefront of railroad transport. However, some people were opposed to his grand plan. Most people thought that others would steal the iron from the construction and run away with it. They also believed that the dangerous engines would scare the people and possibly animals. However, von Rosen still carried out his plans despite the negative notions of the people. Finally, at a Riksdag in 1853 or 1854, it was agreed that railroads were needed. The railroads of Sweden have given so much towards the positive shift of population count. They also

helped with the trade of Swedish goods.

Chapter Six
Politics

Louis De Geer was the man who proposed the reorganization of the Riksdag. He was convinced that justice demanded the removal of the Estates, even though he was part of the highest Estate in the country. With his leadership, he constructed the reorganization of the Riksdag to be composed of two chambers instead of the four Estates.

Now the Riksdag is made of two chambers. The First Chamber is composed of elected men by the county councils and the different municipalities. They were the "representatives of education and wealth." Men are the only ones eligible to be a part of this chamber. Other criteria include their age, income, and wealth. The Second Chamber is composed of men and voters who have their own real property or are able to pay tax on an annual basis. This paved the way for Sweden's present political system.

However, this system only catered to men. For years, it has only been men who had a say in the country's political landscape. By 1884, the first motion for women's equal political rights was brought to the Riksdag's attention. However, it was not passed. They tried again in 1912, but to no avail.

Although, a movement for women's suffrage was forming outside Riksdag. And when the revolution started along with the aftermath of the First World War, the Riksdag approved of the equal suffrage of both men and women. In 1912, five women were allowed to have a seat in the Riksdag.

However, there were still some requirements for eligibility to vote. One of them was that men had to have been part of the military. Of course, this was taken down in 1922, following the agreement of Riksdag. Another requirement to be able to vote is that individuals should not have gone bankrupt or be dependent on economic support. However, again, this requirement was abolished by 1945.

Sweden is now a Constitutional Monarchy. Its constitution follows the four fundamental laws: The Instrument of Government, The Act of Succession, The Freedom of the Press Act, and The Riksdag. The constitution is also based on popular sovereignty, representative democracy, and parliamentarian principles. The monarch has no real political power, and their responsibilities are purely ceremonial. The next heir would be the firstborn child, regardless of the child's gender. The Riksdag decides on the prime minister after talking to the different party leaders. Then the prime minister selects his/her cabinet members. Meanwhile, the prime minister's duties don't involve the legislation's administration details. Those duties are being taken care of by the central administrative agencies. These agencies have senior officials appointed by the cabinet.

The Riksdag is a parliament elected by the people every four years. It is the foundation for democracy in Sweden's politics. The Riksdag appoints the speakers, deputy speakers, and standing committees. Further down the administrative hierarchy, there are local governments in each municipality responsible for their own streets, sewage systems, water supply, schools, public assistance, child welfare, housing, and elderly welfare. Their elections are held together with the parliamentary elections. In addition, right between the national government and the municipal government are the counties ruled by a county governor, who the federal government appoints. Every country has its own council that has the right to get taxes and aid in health care, educational and vocational training, and its own regional transport.

There used to be a party system in Sweden, in which major parties included the nonsocialist parties. There is the Moderate party (formerly known as Conservative Party), the Centre Party, the Liberal Party, and the Green Party. The other two prominent parties are socialist parties: the Swedish Democratic Workers' Party (also known as SAP) and the Left Party (formerly the Communist Party). However, at the start of the 21st century, the parties boiled down into two: The Social Democrats and the Moderates.

Are You Enjoying Reading?

As an independent publisher

with a tiny marketing budget

we rely on readers, like you.

If you're receiving help from this book,

would you please take a moment to write a brief review?

We really appreciate it.

Chapter Seven
Society

To better understand the history of politics, it is a must to answer three great social questions. Social progress is the fuel for political change.

The first was women's rights. The face of women's rights in Sweden was Fredrika Bremer. Her writing profession accorded high respect, but her ambition in life was to destroy constraint and repression for her sisters. In 1894, she went to America and stayed there for two years, familiarizing herself with the institutions for women's rights. When she came back to Sweden, she started to write again. But not as a novelist; she became a writer for social reform. With joy, she started to teach in schools for women. She was able to create a women's center called the Fredrika Bremer Association, which aims to support women in moral, intellectual, social, and economic aspects.

The next topic for social progress in Sweden is the Temperance Movement. During the days of Gustavus III to the middle of the nineteenth century, alcoholism increased at a worrisome rate. Drinking alcohol during meals was a common practice and to get drunk back then wasn't taboo. Even coming into work drunk was normal.

The man who helped Sweden get sober was Peter Wieselgren, a pastor who began the Temperance Movement and believed drunkenness was an evil that should be stopped. He started this movement through his sermons and then visited homes to preach. He was met with resistance and was even a target of assassination. One day, one of the people who wanted him dead invited Wieselgren into his home, claiming that his wife was on the brink of death and needed help. Wieselgren, despite warnings, went anyway. When he arrived, he saw a woman in bed, in pain. He asked her to stand up, and she did. Suddenly, her pain was gone, and when Wieselgren turned around, the man had an ax, ready to kill. Wieselgren told him to put it down, and the peasant did so. He then urged the man to confess and ask God for forgiveness, but the peasant refused, saying he would only do that if he were dying. Karma was on the job because, after a few days, the peasant fell into a well and drowned. He was drunk at the time. Because of this, Wieselgren's next sermon had a powerful impact on the people, and soon, they started to respect and accept his mission. Slowly, the Movement spread throughout the country, and even the crowned prince renounced alcohol.

In 1854, the Riksdag elected to curb the operations of private distilleries, requiring all large and taxed distilleries to have a permit to continue their production. Because of this change, the crime rate went down, and many Swedish were saved from embarrassing deaths because of alcohol poisoning.

The last issue on the topic of social progress in Sweden is labor. Sweden is not exempted from labor problems. There were strikes and lockouts. Social and industrial organizations adopted the United States' example and fought to protect the worker's health, women and child labor regulations, and insurance. In 1913, the Riksdag passed the Act for General People's Pensions granting pension to those required, no matter what gender they are, to stop working at the age of 67. However, the criminals (such as drunkards) aren't given this right.

Pictured above is a gathering for Women Suffrage in Sweden.

This is a picture of Louis de Geer.

Chapter Eight

Literature

The Period of New Romanticism in Sweden delivered poetry and song. Johan Olof Wallin was an artist whose style was very close to Romanticism but never joined the ranks of that period's elite poets. He was a hymnist and preacher born in Dalecarlia from humble beginnings. When he was young, he struggled against poverty and bad health. But he was able to power through all these obstacles. He died as the archbishop of the kingdom. Wallin made a Swedish Hymn book in 1819, and his most notable poem is called "The Angel of Death."

The Gothic Society was organized in 1811 in Stockholm by patriotic youths from Farmland. The Society's goal is to learn the old Gothic love of freedom, courage, and sincerity. Per Henrik Ling, one of the founders of the Gothic Society, was a historian who received the nickname of "the Asa-bard and champion." Like most influential men, he was the minister's son. However, he lost his parents at a young age. This caused him to grow up faster than most. He wasn't the healthiest kid, so he turned to fencing and gymnastics to boost his physical health. Physical activities helped him realize the benefits of exercise. He would spread his discovery everywhere, making people listen to his theory. He studied anatomy, and from there, developed a system of gymnastics that made sure every muscle in the body would have equal exercise. Because of this, he became the founder of gymnastics who believed it was a real form of art.

Erik Gustaf Geijer was an eager athlete because of his younger years. However, he was first known as a poet. Some of his works include *The Viking, The Freeholder, The Charcoal Boy*, and *The Last Scaled*. He was a composer as well. However, besides all this, he was most known as a historian. He wrote the book entitled *History of Swedish People* as a tribute to and to document the history of their forefathers.

Esaias Tegnér ran away from a toxic household and found a job as an assistant secretary to the crown official. His boss saw Tegnér's love for books and reading and his gift of writing. Because of this, opportunities arose for the young Esaias to get an education. With determination, he was marked as a remarkable student. His first patriotic poem was entitled "Svea." The poem was so outstanding that the Swedish Academy recognized him. When he was 42, he was given the role of Bishop of Vixiö and served for 22 years until he died.

A new period for literature came after the year 1860. Viktor Rydberg was one of the artists at this time. He led a sad childhood, but his artistic gifts carried him out of the slump. For the children of Sweden, he was known as the writer of *Little Vigg's Adventures on Christmas Eve, The Freebooter on the Baltic*, and *Singolla*. The best poem he made is most likely the *Cantata*.

Another artist from this period was Carl Snoilsky. He followed the footsteps of Runeberg and Topelius. He wrote *Swedish Pictures*, which talks about the praises of heroic actions and peaceful achievements on the battlefield.

Realism and Idealism came to Sweden around 1880. Realism was all about the misery and sadness of society. So, most art was very pessimistic. Towards the end of Realism, they believed that Romanticism was gone. However, its influence is still there. Sentimentalism was gone, but the thought of eternal life was still there.

Chapter Nine

Other Arts and Architecture

Painting came to the North at a slow pace. It wasn't until contemporary times did Sweden start producing many painters. Despite their late start, Sweden has made a name for itself with distinguished painters such as Georg von Rosen, Gustaf Cederström, and so much more. Georg von Rosen's paintings are focused on history. His goal was to express the truth of its characters. His most celebrated painting is *Eric XIV*, which showed the anguish of Eric. Gustaf Cederström is another Sweden historical painter. His most famous work is called *Funeral procession of King Charles XII,* where he used somber hues instead of vibrant colors

Julius Kronberg has the alias "A Poet of Colors." He was famous among the children of Sweden because of his artwork of the Bible stories. He also shared his art to help the architecture of the city, painting a number of ceilings in public buildings across Sweden. He was also a portrait painter. Prince Eugene was a nature painter creating a collection of moments in nature, such as lights during the evenings or the summer nights. In comparison, Bruno Liljefors was a painter of wildlife. He specifically depicted animals in deep forests, plains, or the ocean's shores. Karl Nordström was a landscape painter. However, he solely focused on the western shores of his country. He was enticed by the scenery of the sea, its cliffs, and rocks. And like Prince Eugene, he preferred to depict the subdued light of the evening rather than any other time of the day.

Carl Larsson is one of the most famous Swedish painters. With his optimism evident in his work, he usually painted moments of home life happiness. Anders Zorn is another famous Swedish painter. He is known to have mastered the art of transferring life to the blank canvas using light and shadow.

Besides painting, there is architecture. The noted Swedish architects are Isak Gustaf Clason, Ferdinand Boberg, and Ragnar Östberg. Clason's best masterpiece is the Northern Museum, a solid art reflecting real national character. Clason is the face of modern Swedish architecture. At the same time, Boberg is all about new architectural forms to express personality. A building that Boberg made is the post office building in Stockholm. Scandinavian architecture gained traction in the early decades of the 20th century, giving birth to Swedish Grace, a style that is a mix between Neoclassicism and traditional elements. A notable structure at this time was the Stockholm City Hall, created by Ragnar Östberg in 1932. Another famous building is the Stockholm Public Library, designed by Gunnar Asplund in 1928.

As time passed, Functionalism (also known as Funkis) became the most prevalent style in Swedish architecture. It works by combining minimal aesthetics with humanistic quality. An example of this style is the Woodland Cemetery built by Gunnar Asplund and Sigurd Lewerentz. Another is St. Mark's Church, created by Lewerentz as well.

Architecture and art go hand in hand as they both create beautiful products from almost close to nothing.

Chapter Ten

Notable Names in Science and Discoveries

Science is the foundation of growth in almost every aspect of life. These Swedes revolutionized the world, and not just their country.

Jöns Jakob Berzelius was born into poverty. He lost both his parents and was adopted by his other family members. Despite this, he was able to become a professor at the Carolinian Institute in Stockholm, focusing on chemistry. He invented the system of notation for chemistry that helped Carl Linnæus in his botanical research.

John Ericsson grew up together with his brother Nils Ericson, the mechanical engineer who built the Swedish railways. He decided to go to the Promised Land of England to do his work with mechanics and industrial projects. In England, he made several inventions, including the propeller. But for some reason, the British people didn't accept his inventions. So, Ericsson left England and headed for the United States. When he arrived in the United States, he was given the go signal to help construct a war vessel with a propeller. It was a success and forever changed the blueprint of naval transport internationally. However, even with all these praises, Ericsson kept humility. He continued working while maintaining a low profile, making new inventions. His work was his life. He earned profit from his experiments and helping people in poverty. However, even though he was in the United States, his love for his country remained.

Alfred B. Nobel is a Swedish engineer who invented dynamite, one of the most destructive, powerful objects man has ever created; only if in the right hands, it's one of the best inventions of all time. Other engineering inventions, such as railway tunnels and the canal construction, could have never been possible without labor, expense, and dynamite. It changed the world. Nobel died on December 10, 1896, entrusting the proceeds of his estate to a fund. This fund would later be allocated to people who have given unprecedented contributions to mankind's progress each year. The endowment fund encompasses works that have benefited the human race in terms of Physics, Chemistry, Medicine, Literature, and Peace. This was the beginning of the illustrious "Nobel Prize." Today, this fund is managed by a board of directors appointed by the Swedish government.

In the minds of the Swedish, the Viking expeditions and their love for adventure are innate. Adolf Erik Nordenskiöld, the most famous Swedish explorer of the last century, was no stranger to this love. A professor of Mineralogy in Stockholm, he did many northern expeditions and located Spitzbergen. He went even further, going into the interior of Greenland and explored its uncharted territory more than any explorer has ever done before him. He studied polar ice fields and arctic currents. Because of this, he discovered that there was open water in Northern Asia which then helped the circumnavigation of the Old World of Europe, Asia, and Africa, connecting routes that formed the basis of modern cross-ocean travel. In the year 1878, Nordenskiöld brought three ships with him to go through the narrow channels between the icefields and the coast of Asia. Despite the hardships, he continued his expedition. However, he passed away while traversing the Bering Strait.

Today, the face of modern Swedish exploration is Sven Hedin. He led expeditions to Central Asia. While he struggled throughout his life because of these expeditions, he succeeded in cartographing places and regions that were unknown until he came along.

This is the Interior of Stockholm's Public Library.

This is the exterior of the Church at Kiruna.

Chapter Eleven

Aftermath of World Wars One and Two

The aftermath of the First World War had an impact on the whole world and naturally, on Swedish society. However, as a neutral country, it wasn't about death and destruction for them. The effect on them was more on the economic and political side of the coin.

The year 1918 came to be known as the birth of Modern Sweden. Even though there was bitterness over emergency national regulation and legislation, the war affected reforms on Sweden's institutions, such as the church, civil society, and some local authorities, and World War I became a catalyst for the nationalization of Sweden. Agriculture and labor continued. Appointments of new authorities like the National Health Authorities were set up. The Elementary and Grammar School reforms of 1919 and 1927 helped the government reestablish its education system. The nationalization of the local authorities started in 1925 because they had to appease the military and the violent militias.

The war also helped the central government get a tighter grip on their economic responsibilities and the welfare of the country's people. Sweden made a new taxation system that allowed the development of the public welfare system, specifically allocating allowances for families with children, and complemented this with social reforms like free school meals, maternal support, healthcare in school, and the like. They also had pro-natalist policies because of the decline in their birth rates. Public health care was given priority as well.

The war also changed the Swedish political scene. It helped speed up the democratization process, and the country became inclusive under the pressure of radical movements. Other important, big effects of war from the political standpoint are the political reforms that were at first blocked but are now resolved. They also had a constitutional reform for universal and equal suffrage, the reign of the parliament, and consultative referendums.

However, the war also highlighted the divide between the social classes. Because of this, the Farmers' Party was established in 1921. Being the neutral country, or the "spectator" of World War I, has gotten Sweden to look more inward and examine its society. The war, however tragic, helped Sweden assess its internal political and economic problems and helped fix most of them.

After World War II, the government of Stockholm accepted that war criminals were to be banished from their country. However, they also claimed that there were no war criminals in their land. Towards the end of the war, there were a large number of refugees who came to Sweden looking for safety. However, the Swedish authorities became paranoid that they might be spies for the Nazis. What they did next was to question all of them once they arrived in Sweden. There were no exceptions for this process. Because of this, Sweden didn't exactly know which of the refugees were actual war criminals seeking safety in a neutral territory.

At the end of it all, it is evident that Sweden has a knack for negotiations. They stayed "publicly" neutral after all.

This is a monument made for Albin Hansson.

Chapter Twelve
Conclusion

Learning the history of any country is imperative when you want to form a legitimate opinion about them. You can't just have an idea on a topic without knowing where they come from first. Based on Sweden's history, how do you feel about the country now?

Sweden's history is so rich, owing to its intertwined history with Denmark and Norway (especially Denmark). The fact that they've had so much history together says something about their core national philosophies. It makes you wonder about all the times anyone formed an alliance because of a shared past, kind of like when people bond over the same enemy. "The enemy of my enemy is my friend," as the saying goes. What is evident in Sweden's history is the perseverance of its people. If you look closely, everything they've done is to ensure their country's safety and liberty. They fought for Sweden, no matter the consequences. However, there are just a select few that are not as nationalistic as the rest; there will always be villains in a land full of heroes. In general, Swedish people are so loyal to their country and have a great love for it.

When it came to the World Wars, Sweden's facade was of neutrality. But internally, they struggled. This shows that your public self is different from your true self. Even if you appear indifferent on the outside, there will always be turmoil about who you really are inside. To the eyes of the world, Sweden was officially neutral, but its internal structure violently shook as its factions chose sides. Some people support the Germans, and others don't. This became a constant battle, and unless you've reached self-actualization, no one can end the war inside.

Choices. These, ideally, are always backed up with sound reason and logic. Some reasons are uncontestable, like solid evidence. Then some reasons need convincing, like how you have a gut feeling about something. In relation to the history of Sweden during the World Wars, some people supported Germany because of its ties with the country, a reason based on emotions, not logic. Taking Sweden's case, you must learn to filter out noise and form concrete judgment before choosing a road. "Emotions cloud judgment" is too true of a saying.

What you should get from this is that internal struggles are not only applicable to people but also to countries. Sweden is a good example of that. Also, you should always learn to be informed before you make an opinion. Knowing more details can always help you make an informed opinion, possibly even a good one. And finally, you should learn that you need to be practical when it comes to your choices. Weigh out the pros and cons of a decision. You can't just rely on your gut alone. Logic is there for a reason. Use it. And you will be able to turn the tides into your favor.

Chapter Thirteen

Discussion Question

St. Ansgar was someone who tried to spread Christianity through Sweden as peacefully as possible. And the Swedish people allowed him to preach, even if they didn't convert just yet. Will you ever let someone preach and convert people in your country while you believe in your own religion? Will you stop them or let them preach freely?

Discussion Question

The Christians were ruthless in their Crusades. They wanted people to convert to Christianity. If you were them, and wanted to preach your religion (including atheism or agnosticism), would you go to such lengths to convert other people? Why do you think the Crusades resorted to brute force?

Discussion Question

Alcoholism isn't new to us. We still have it around the world. Do you think the way they handled alcoholism in Sweden was the best way? Would you have done it differently?

Discussion Question

From the Four Estates, the Riksdag reformed to the Two Chambers.

One chamber was represented by the rich, and the other was

represented by the lower classes. If you were to reform the Riksdag,

would you stick with this system? If not, how would you do it?

Discussion Question

John Ericsson went to another country to be able to make his inventions. This outsourcing isn't new to us at present. Some people move to other countries for various pursuits. Would you ever move to another country for your occupation? Why and why not?

Discussion Question

Realism is all about the truth of life's pessimism. Romanticism, however, is all about the optimistic life. What do you think is better when it comes to art?

Discussion Question

Sweden claimed that they were neutral during wars. If you were in the middle of a fight between two friends, would you say your side or stay neutral? Why would you do what you will do?

Discussion Question

Neutrality is Sweden's go-to action in war (based on the first two wars). Will you ever accept this action? Why do you think Sweden wanted to be neutral?

Chapter Fourteen
Quiz Question

1. **True/False:** Scandinavia was composed of three countries at first. These countries include Denmark, Norway and Sweden. However, Iceland and Finland joined later on, forming the Nordic countries.

2. **True/False:** The Kalmar Union was started by Queen Margaret of Denmark, who believed the three kingdoms will be more powerful if they are merged together. The three kingdoms are: Denmark, Sweden and Norway.

3. **True/False:** The Riksdag was first composed of Two Estates. However, it was reformed to be composed of Four Chambers. The Chambers are divided by social class.

4. **True/False:** There were three topics of importance in the social progress of Sweden. One is about women and their rights. The second is about the Temperance Movement, which is about alcoholism. And the last is about the labor conditions in the country and how it was unfair.

5. **True/ False:** The propeller was invented by John Ericsson. He created it overseas because he didn't have resources back in Sweden. Because of this invention, he revolutionized the navy ships.

6. **True/False:** The art form of painting came in before the art of poetry in Sweden. Some of the poets of Sweden were hymnists as well. Some painters, on the other hand, use nature as their muse.

7. **True/False:** The Midsummer Crisis of Sweden was because of a decoded message Germany made to Berlin. In that message, they said they plan to invade Sweden, despite their "leave traffic" deal. The crisis was about what Sweden should do as their next step.

8. **True/ False:** Sweden openly sided with Germany in World War II. However, they were neutral during the First World War. This was a tipping point for the war.

Quiz Answer

1. True

2. False. Queen Margaret was from Sweden, not Denmark.

3. False. There were Four Estates, and then, it was reformed into Two Chambers.

4. True

5. . True

6. False. Poetry came faster to Swedish culture, not painting.

7. True

8. False. Sweden was publicly neutral during World Wars I and II.

Bonus Downloads

*Get Free Books with **<u>Any Purchase</u>** History Shorts*

Every purchase comes with a FREE download!

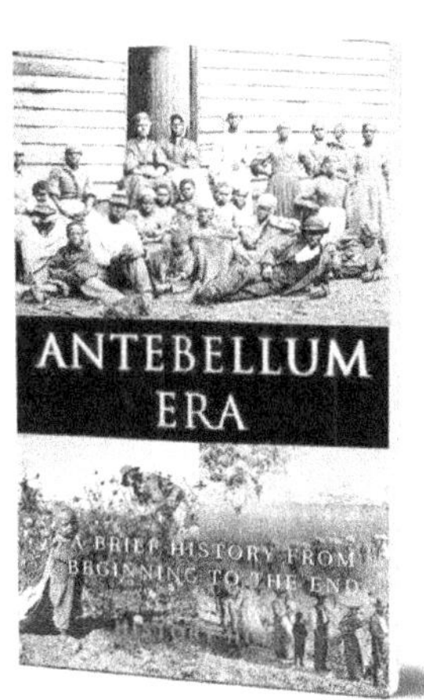